MAKE ME THE BEST

BASKETBALL PLAYER

BY WILL GRAVES

SportsZone

An Imprint of Abdo Publishing
abdopublishing.com

abdopublishing.com

Published by Abdo Publishing, a division of ABDO, PO Box 398166, Minneapolis, Minnesota 55439. Copyright © 2017 by Abdo Consulting Group, Inc. International copyrights reserved in all countries. No part of this book may be reproduced in any form without written permission from the publisher. SportsZone™ is a trademark and logo of Abdo Publishing.

Printed in the United States of America, North Mankato, Minnesota
082016
012017

THIS BOOK CONTAINS
RECYCLED MATERIALS

Cover Photos: Christopher Futcher/iStockphoto, top left; Shutterstock Images, top right, middle left; Steve Debenport/iStockphoto, bottom left; Tony Dejak/AP Images, bottom right
Interior Photos: Christopher Futcher/iStockphoto, 4, (top left); Shutterstock Images, 4 (middle left), 4–5 (top); Steve Debenport/iStockphoto, 4 (bottom left); Tony Dejak/ AP Images, 4–5 (bottom); Marcio Jose Sanchez/AP Images, 7, 11, 37, 43; Ann Heisenfelt/ AP Images, 8; Ben Margot/AP Images, 13; Alex Gallardo/AP Images, 15; Mark J. Terrill/AP Images, 16, 19; Eric Gay/AP Images, 22; David J. Phillip/AP Images, 21; Rich Pedroncelli/ AP Images, 25; Stephen Lew/Cal Sport Media/AP Images, 27, 31; Max Becherer/AP Images, 28; J. P. Wilson/Icon Sportswire/AP Images, 32–33; Sue Ogrocki/AP Images, 34; Ross D. Franklin/AP Images, 39; Ron Schwane/AP Images, 40; Tony Dejak/AP Images, 45

Editor: Patrick Donnelly
Series Designer: Nikki Farinella
Content Consultant: Brad Schaper, Head Boys' Basketball Coach, Luther High School, Onalaska, Wisconsin

Publisher's Cataloging-in-Publication Data

Names: Graves, Will, author.
Title: Make me the best basketball player / by Will Graves.
Description: Minneapolis, MN : Abdo Publishing, 2017. | Series: Make me the best athlete | Includes bibliographical references and index.
Identifiers: LCCN 2016945688 | ISBN 9781680784879 (lib. bdg.) | ISBN 9781680798159 (ebook)
Subjects: LCSH: Basketball--Juvenile literature.
Classification: DDC 796.323--dc23
LC record available at http://lccn.loc.gov/2016945688

TABLE OF

CONTENTS

INTRODUCTION

The biggest stars in the National Basketball Association (NBA) can make it look so easy.

Stephen Curry pulls up from somewhere near midcourt to let a three-pointer fly. Chris Paul weaves through big men in the lane before finding an open teammate for an easy basket. Russell Westbrook blows by a defender on his way to the basket. LeBron James does all the things that make him one of the best players on the planet.

Yet all of the game's greats were just like you once. James didn't always rack up triple-doubles whenever he felt like it. Curry didn't always knock down threes without breaking a sweat.

It took time, good coaching, lots of practice, and maybe even a little luck for these players to reach the top. So let's take it one step at a time. Even Michael Jordan had to learn how to dribble before he could fly.

SHOOT LIKE

STEPHEN CURRY

Stephen Curry doesn't look like most professional basketball players. At 6 feet 3 inches, he's not very tall. At 190 pounds, he's not very big. And he's got a bit of a baby face. He might be mistaken for a teenager hanging around the local gym, not one of the greatest shooters in NBA history. But the Golden State Warriors sharpshooter learned at a young age that proper form and a little imagination can help you score against even the toughest defenders.

Curry set an NBA record with 402 three-pointers made during the 2015–16 season. That broke the record of 286 he set the year before.

Curry's father, Dell Curry, spent 16 years in the NBA as one of the best shooters in the league. Having worked tirelessly on his fundamentals, Stephen Curry

Stephen Curry displays his perfect form against the Cleveland Cavaliers in the 2016 NBA Finals.

is comfortable shooting from anywhere. The NBA three-point line is 23 feet, 9 inches from the basket. Curry has no problem letting it go from 30 feet away or more. In 2015 and again in 2016 he was named

Curry's daughter Riley is a bit of a star herself. Clips of the toddler joining her dad for postgame interviews went viral during the 2015 playoffs.

SHOOT LIKE STEPHEN CURRY

- Make sure you are square to the basket. That means your head, shoulders, hips, and feet are all facing the same way.

- Bend your knees. Your legs provide power and balance.

- Put your shooting hand underneath the ball. Place your other hand on the side of the ball. Your shooting hand provides the push, while your guide hand makes sure the ball flies straight.

- "Reach for the Peach." The first basketball hoops were peach baskets hung on a wall. After you release the ball at the top of your jump, extend your arm toward the rim and bend your wrist, like you are reaching into a peach basket.

- Develop a routine. For example, some players dribble the ball three times before shooting free throws. Whatever your routine, try to do it every time so your body becomes comfortable and you get a feel for what the right shot is for you.

Even with a hand in his face, Curry's fundamentals stay true.

NBA Most Valuable Player (MVP) while setting league records for three-pointers attempted and made each year.

The three-pointer has become an important shot in basketball during the last 30 years. Teams that have good three-point shooters force the defense to guard them far away from the basket. That opens up the court for other players. Before the three-pointer came along, teams

///////// **Curry's younger brother, Seth Curry, became a regular contributor for the Sacramento Kings in the 2015–16 season.**

LARRY BIRD

Larry Bird entered the NBA in 1979, the same year the league introduced the three-pointer. It was a match made in basketball heaven. Bird became one of the first players to take full advantage of the new shot. "Larry Legend" twice led the league in three-pointers during his Hall of Fame career. He also won the three-point contest held during NBA All-Star weekend three times. Before the 1988 All-Star contest, Bird asked the rest of the players, "Who's finishing second?" Then he went out and won it. On his last shot, Bird held his right arm high in the air in triumph as the ball dropped through the net.

The two-time MVP is a huge hit with Warriors fans.

often packed their defense near the lane, which slowed the game down.

Curry's greatness is not limited to long-distance shooting. He's also one of the best free-throw shooters in the league because he's so consistent. Curry's jump shot looks the same whether he's throwing in 30-foot rainbows or 10-footers in the lane. Because his form is the same every time, he only needs to worry about how much power to put into his shot.

Curry was born in Akron, Ohio, in the same hospital where LeBron James was born.

DRILL DOWN!

This catch-and-shoot drill will work up a sweat.

1. Two players stand in the same spot, both facing the basket. Player A takes a jump shot, then follows the ball to the hoop.

2. Player A grabs the rebound before it hits the ground, if possible, passes it to Player B, and runs to a different spot on the court.

3. Player B shoots, gets the rebound, passes it to Player A, and follows the pass.

4. Player A shoots, rebounds, passes, and moves to a new spot. Continue for a set number of repetitions.

PASS LIKE

CHRIS PAUL

Chris Paul spent part of his childhood working at a gas station owned by his grandfather, whom he called "PaPa Chili." Sometimes PaPa Chili would let customers fill up and pay him back later if they didn't have the money at the time.

PaPa Chili's acts of generosity stuck with Paul as he grew up in North Carolina. Though he was lightning quick with the ball in his hands and could get to the hoop whenever he wanted, Paul loved to set up his teammates for easy shots.

Paul won two Olympic gold medals while playing point guard for Team USA at the 2008 and 2012 Summer Games.

Paul brought that mindset with him to the NBA in 2005. He quickly became one of the league's elite passers, using his court vision and

Chris Paul is one of the NBA's most dynamic passers.

basketball smarts to make sure every player on his team became involved on offense.

Passing is the hallmark of any good team, because it forces the defense to be on the move constantly. If one player just

Paul is a pretty good defender, too. He has led the NBA in steals six times and was named to the NBA All-Defensive first team on six occasions.

PASS LIKE CHRIS PAUL

- Keep your head up. The best passers see the entire court, not just the player defending them.

- To throw a chest pass, hold the ball at your chest, step toward your target, extend your arms, and push the ball where you want it to go. Finish the pass with your thumbs down and palms out.

- A bounce pass involves stepping toward your target and bouncing the ball off the court more than halfway to your teammate. The ball should still be coming up when it reaches their hands.

- Use a baseball pass when your teammate is far away. Lift the ball over your head and cock your arm back, just like you do when you're throwing a baseball. Take a step with your opposite foot and let it fly.

Paul keeps his head up and his options open when he's running the Los Angeles Clippers offense.

Paul's nickname (CP3) isn't just a reference to his jersey number. His father and older brother also have the initials C. P., making Chris "CP3."

dribbles while his teammates stand around, the game becomes slow and predictable. The more an offense remains in motion, the more likely a player will get open for a shot.

BOB COUSY

In the early days of basketball, players were less creative and took fewer chances on the court. As a result, passing was predictable. Bob Cousy changed all that. The Boston Celtics guard turned passing into an art form. During his Hall of Fame career from 1951 to 1963, Cousy was a showman. He was the first to perfect the no-look pass and the behind-the-back dribble, skills that helped him lead the NBA in assists for eight straight seasons. It's not a coincidence the Celtics won six league titles with Cousy running the show.

DRILL DOWN!

The three-player weave works well with chest or bounce passes.

1. Three players stand on the baseline: Player A under the hoop, Player B on the right, and Player C on the left.

2. As the players move forward, Player A passes to Player B and follows the pass, running behind Player B.

3. Player B passes to Player C and follows the pass, running behind Player C, who then passes to Player A.

4. Continue down the court passing and following the ball until the last player makes a layup.

REBOUND LIKE

DWIGHT HOWARD

Dwight Howard is not Superman. But the 6-foot-11 center does a reasonable impersonation of his favorite superhero.

Like Superman, sometimes Howard can fly. During the 2008 NBA Slam Dunk contest, Howard donned a Superman T-shirt and a red cape. Then, he soared high for a thunderous jam that earned him a perfect score and the slam dunk title.

Howard was named the co-MVP of the 2004 McDonald's All-American Game. The annual contest features the best high school players in the country.

Dunking helped make Howard famous. But rebounding made him great. The Orlando Magic made Howard the top pick in the 2004 NBA Draft when he was just 18 years old. He was big, strong, and fast.

Using two hands, Dwight Howard rips a rebound away from Golden State's Draymond Green.

Rebounding is one of basketball's most important jobs. Good defensive teams are usually good rebounding teams. And offensive rebounding creates additional chances to score.

At age 23, Howard became the youngest player ever to lead the NBA in rebounds in 2007–08. The next year he was the youngest to lead the league in blocked shots.

Howard led the NBA in rebounding five times between 2008 and 2013. The league also named him the Defensive Player of the Year three times because of the

REBOUND LIKE DWIGHT HOWARD

- Get in position. Being in the right spot when the ball comes off the rim will give you an edge over other players.

- Box out. Keep your feet shoulder-width apart, bend your knees, and extend your arms to the side. This will protect the space you've created underneath the basket.

- Anticipate the shot. If you're playing away from the basket and you see a player get into shooting position, don't hesitate—be aggressive and crash the boards. Getting a brief head start could be the difference between grabbing and missing a rebound.

"Superman" can dunk, but Dwight Howard's rebounding makes him truly elite.

way he dominated under the hoop. During his best years, Howard's shot-blocking skills nearly matched his elite rebounding abilities.

In 2009 Howard led the Magic to the NBA Finals. They lost to the Los Angeles Lakers, but it would be hard to blame Howard for the defeat. He averaged 15.3 rebounds per game during Orlando's playoff run. His outstanding play lifted the Magic to the finals for the second time in team history.

CHARLES BARKLEY

Charles Barkley didn't fit the mold of most great rebounders. Although he was officially listed at 6-foot-6, he claimed he was closer to 6-4. He had a thick body, too, earning him the nickname "The Round Mound of Rebound." That size hardly mattered during his Hall of Fame career. Barkley was an expert at finding his way to missed shots. During 16 NBA seasons, Barkley averaged at least 10 rebounds every season except one. In 1987 he became the shortest player in NBA history to lead the league in rebounding.

DRILL DOWN!

This exercise will help improve your offensive rebounding and scoring in the post.

1. Stand on the baseline just to the right of the hoop.

2. Throw the ball off the backboard. Instead of grabbing the rebound, tap it back up on the backboard with your right hand.

3. Tap it nine times. On the tenth time, try to tap it into the hoop.

4. Switch hands and repeat the process on the left side with your left hand.

BLOCK SHOTS LIKE

ANTHONY DAVIS

While growing up in Chicago, Anthony Davis seemed an unlikely candidate to become one of the best shot blockers the NBA has ever seen.

Davis played guard during most of his childhood. But a 10-inch growth spurt in high school changed his life.

////////// **Davis has a twin sister named Antoinette. His older sister, Iesha, played hoops at Richard J. Daley College.**

By the time he was a senior, Davis was 6-foot-10 with long arms. His wingspan—the measurement from fingertip to fingertip with your arms spread wide—was 89 inches (2.3 m). That's more than 7 feet! He could easily touch the net without jumping.

But you need more than height to block shots. A great sense of timing helps, too. You don't want to get called

Anthony Davis shows the importance of going straight up when blocking a shot.

for a foul while trying to swat a shot into the stands. All those years playing guard helped Davis when he became a power forward. He understands better than most big players how plays develop. He uses his basketball smarts to anticipate where the ball is going, and he leaps off the floor to knock it away.

Davis set a major-college record for blocks in a season by a freshman during his one year at Kentucky. He blocked 186 shots in 40 games.

BLOCK SHOTS LIKE ANTHONY DAVIS

- Keep your hands up. It's impossible to block a shot if your hands are by your side!

- Put your arms straight up. If you lean forward, even if you don't make contact with the shooter, the refs are likely to call a foul. Try to block the shot using your hand that's closest to the ball.

- Keep moving. Running out at a shooter with your arms extended can be enough to alter an opponent's form. Even if you don't block the shot, you still might cause them to miss it.

Davis gets off the ground to block San Antonio Spurs center Tim Duncan's shot.

A great shot blocker can be a key part of a strong team defense. Opponents will be less likely to challenge you inside and instead will settle for lower-percentage outside shots if you have a strong presence like Davis guarding the rim. He led the NBA in blocks during the 2013–14 season and did it again a year later.

DIKEMBE MUTOMBO

Dikembe Mutombo's right index finger got a workout during the 7-foot-2 center's long NBA career. Mutombo, who led the league in blocks three times, often celebrated after a block by wagging his right finger at an opponent as if to say "no, no, no." He was named the NBA Defensive Player of the Year four times. He retired in 2009 with 3,289 career blocks, the second most in NBA history.

DRILL DOWN!

This exercise can help your awareness and reaction time.

1. One defensive player stands in the middle of the lane. Two offensive players line up on either side of the lane.

2. A teammate or coach at the top of the key passes the ball to one of the offensive players.

3. The player with the ball gets one step to get to the basket and attempt a shot. The defensive player slides over and tries to prevent the shot.

4. Repeat the process on either side.

DRIVE LIKE

RUSSELL WESTBROOK

Unlike most point guards, Russell Westbrook isn't known for his passing. He's not even famous for his shooting. He's good at both of those skills, but he's best known for using his speed and power to get to the basket for easy shots.

Being able to blow past a defender and drive to the hoop is an important skill to master. If you beat your man using the dribble, another player will have to shift over to guard you. Then the rest of the defense has to scramble, and that usually leaves one of your teammates open. A strong drive also gives you the option of getting all the way to the basket, where you can get a layup or a dunk or maybe draw a foul.

////////// Westbrook posted 18 triple-doubles during the 2015–16 season, the most in the NBA.

Russell Westbrook beats Stephen Curry on a drive to the hoop.

The Oklahoma City Thunder chose Westbrook with the fourth pick in the 2008 NBA Draft and paired him with silky smooth forward Kevin Durant. The two players made a great combination.

Although Westbrook shoots with his right hand, he uses his left to sign autographs, brush his teeth, and do everything else not related to basketball.

DRIVE LIKE RUSSELL WESTBROOK

- Get into in "triple-threat" position on the perimeter to keep the defense guessing. Hold the ball at your hip while in an athletic stance that allows for movement. You now have three options: rise and shoot, pass to a teammate, or dribble.

- Mix in a pump fake to get your defender out of position. Fake a shot, making sure not to leave your feet. When your opponent jumps to block it, pull the ball down and drive to the hoop.

- Keep your head up. You can't see what the defense is doing if you're looking at the ball while you dribble. Keeping your head up also lets you know when a teammate is open.

- Learn how to make a layup with either hand. This skill will keep the defense from guessing which way you are going to drive.

Westbrook takes advantage of the open passing lanes when the defense scrambles to cover him.

Durant became one of the league's best scorers. Opposing defenses focused so much attention on Durant that it gave Westbrook plenty of room to work. Westbrook is nearly unstoppable on the fast break. His combination of speed and power make it difficult for opposing defenders to keep up.

Because he drives to the basket so well, Westbrook draws a lot of fouls. He finished in the top 10 in free-throw attempts five times between 2010–11 and 2015–16.

Durant was a free agent after the 2015–16 season. He signed with the Golden State Warriors. That gave Westbrook the opportunity to expand his offensive skills and leadership abilities.

ALLEN IVERSON

Allen Iverson spent 14 years blowing by defenders on his way to layup after layup. He was a 6-foot blur as he slashed into the lane, leaving opponents grasping at air. Iverson was not afraid of anyone. One night he famously shook loose from Chicago Bulls star Michael Jordan and knocked down a jump shot after his crossover dribble froze one of the greatest players of all time.

DRILL DOWN!

NBA Hall of Famer George Mikan made this layup drill famous.

1. Stand beneath the basket just to the right of the hoop, facing the baseline.

2. Jump and shoot a layup with your right hand. Make sure to use the backboard.

3. As soon as you land, jump and grab the ball as high as possible. Your jump should take you to the other side of the hoop.

4. Repeat the process from the left side with your left hand. Continue for a set number of repetitions.

DO IT ALL LIKE

LEBRON JAMES

LeBron James grew up in Akron, Ohio, idolizing Michael Jordan. James even started wearing No. 23, Jordan's number with the Chicago Bulls, to honor his hero. Choosing No. 23 hardly made James stand out. In those days, everybody wanted to "be like Mike," as Jordan's Gatorade commercial used to say.

James's two sons, LeBron Jr. and Bryce, are following in their father's footsteps on the court. LeBron Jr. started to get attention from college coaches when he was just 10 years old.

But the way James played made him rise above the crowd. He was so much better than the other kids that he could have bulldozed his way to the basket and scored whenever he wanted. But he didn't. James knew from a young age that he wanted to play in the NBA. He also knew that the truly great NBA

Rebounding has long been one of LeBron James's strengths.

players aren't great at just one thing. So he worked on every part of his game: shooting, rebounding, defense, and passing.

James worried about being called selfish, so he did his best to get all of his teammates involved in the game. That helped James feel comfortable, as if he was in full control of the game. This is a mindset he's

James caught 27 touchdown passes for his high school football team as a junior. He was an All-Ohio selection as a wide receiver but quit before his senior year to focus on basketball.

DO IT ALL LIKE LeBRON JAMES

- Don't focus only on your shooting. Truly great players pay just as much attention to defense and other elements of the game.

- Get your teammates involved. Learn their strengths and do your best to help make them better.

- Move your feet. It sounds easy, but the best players rarely stand still. If the ball is not in your hands on offense, keep the defense working by staying on the move.

- Work on your weaknesses. You probably know what you do well. Spend extra time improving what needs work.

James keeps his teammates involved in the game with his passing skills.

During his time with the Miami Heat, James wore No. 6 to honor LeBron Jr.'s birthday, October 6.

carried throughout his career. *Sports Illustrated* put him on the cover as a teenager and proclaimed him the next Jordan.

Over the course of the next decade, James delivered on that promise. He helped turn the Cleveland Cavaliers into consistent playoff contenders before spending four years with the Miami Heat. Teaming up with Dwyane Wade and Chris Bosh, he led the Heat to two NBA titles. James helped bring their games to new heights along the way.

MAGIC JOHNSON

Although LeBron James wears No. 23 to honor Michael Jordan, a more fitting number for him might be No. 32. That's the number worn by Los Angeles Lakers point guard Earvin "Magic" Johnson during his Hall of Fame career. The 6-foot-9 Johnson could play all five positions. He even started at center in Game 6 of the 1980 NBA Finals when Kareem Abdul-Jabbar was hurt. Johnson finished with 42 points, 15 rebounds, and seven assists as the Lakers defeated the Philadelphia 76ers to win the NBA title.

James has worked hard to improve his jump shot over the years.

James returned to the Cavaliers in the summer of 2014 and formed a new power trio with Kyrie Irving and Kevin Love. The Cavaliers made it all the way to the NBA Finals in 2015 and pushed the Golden State Warriors to six games, even with Irving and Love both out with injuries. James led Cleveland in points, rebounds, assists, and minutes played in one of the greatest Finals performances ever by a player on the losing team.

The next year, James took it one step further. The Cavaliers and Warriors met in the NBA Finals for the second time, and James again showcased his remarkable all-around game. He became the first player in NBA Finals history to lead both teams in points, rebounds, assists, steals, and blocked shots. And he brought the Cavs back from a 3–1 deficit to win the final three games and bring a championship to Cleveland.

In 2004 James and his mother, Gloria, established the LeBron James Family Foundation to help children and single-parent families in need.

DRILL DOWN!

Work on your agility and quickness with this simple drill.

1. Two players line up side-by-side on the baseline. Player B holds two tennis balls.

2. Player B rolls one tennis ball onto the court. Player A chases down the ball, grabs it, and runs it back to the baseline.

3. Player B repeats the process with the second ball, rolling it to a different spot on the floor.

4. Continue for set number of repetitions. Then switch roles.

GLOSSARY

BOX OUT

To establish rebounding position by using one's body to shield an opposing player from the ball or basket.

DRAFT

A system that allows teams to acquire new players coming into a league.

FOUL

Illegal contact with another player during the course of the game.

FUNDAMENTALS

Basic skills or building blocks of the game.

KEY

The free-throw lane and the free-throw circle together.

LANE

The area near the basket between the free-throw line and the baseline.

REBOUND

The act of grabbing any missed shot.

STEAL

Taking the ball away from an offensive player.

THREE-POINTER

Any shot taken behind the three-point line.

TRIPLE-DOUBLE

When a player reaches double figures in three different statistical categories—usually points, rebounds, and assists—in one game.

FOR MORE INFORMATION

BOOKS

Kaplan, Bobby. *BBall Basics for Kids: A Basketball Handbook*. Bloomington, IN; iUniverse, 2012.

Phelps, Richard, with John Walters and Tim Bourret. *Basketball for Dummies*. Hoboken, NJ; John Wiley & Sons, 2011.

Schaller, Bob, with Coach Dave Harnish. *The Everything Kids' Basketball Book: The All-Time Greats, Legendary Teams, Today's Superstars—and Tips on Playing Like a Pro*. Avon, MA; Adams Media, 2015.

WEBSITES

To learn more about basketball, visit **booklinks.abdopublishing.com**. These links are routinely monitored and updated to provide the most current information available.

PLACE TO VISIT

Naismith Memorial Basketball Hall of Fame
1000 Hall of Fame Avenue
Springfield, Massachusetts 01105
(877) 446-6752
www.hoophall.com
A great place to learn about the history of the game, the Naismith Memorial Basketball Hall of Fame is named after Dr. James Naismith, who invented basketball in 1891. The Hall of Fame features interactive exhibits, including skill challenges, live clinics, and shooting contests.

INDEX

ABOUT THE AUTHOR

Will Graves grew up in the suburbs of Washington, DC, trying to beat his dad in games of "H-O-R-S-E." Instead of becoming a great player, Graves learned to write about them for a living. He has spent the last two decades as a sportswriter, covering both college and professional basketball as well as pro football, hockey, and baseball. He lives in Pittsburgh and works for the Associated Press.